Slavery

Researching American History

Introduced and edited by
Pat Perrin

Philadelphia physician Jesse Torrey compiled interviews, narratives and his own first-hand observations in an illustrated book entitled, A Portraiture of Domestic Slavery in the United States. *(1817) This illustration depicts Torrey sitting in a cabin, writing as a black man talks to him.* (Library of Congress, found on http://www.pbs.org/wgbh/aia/)

Discovery Enterprises, Ltd.
Carlisle, Massachusetts

First Edition © Discovery Enterprises, Ltd., Carlisle, MA 2000

ISBN 1-57960-062-X

Library of Congress Catalog Card Number 00-103459

10   9   8   7   6   5   4   3   2   1

Printed in the United States of America

Subject Reference Guide:

Title: *Slavery*
Series*: Researching American History*
edited by Pat Perrin

Nonfiction
Analyzing documents re: Slavery in the United States

Credits:

Cover illustration: Slaves picking cotton.
(Courtesy of Mediasource, Historical Picture Service, Inc.)

Other Illustrations: Courtesy of the Library of Congress, except as otherwise credited where they appear in the book.

Contents

About the Series

Researching American History is a series of books which introduces various topics and periods in our nation's history through the study of primary source documents.

Reading the Historical Documents

On the following pages you'll find words written by people during or soon after the time of the events. This is firsthand information about what life was like back then. Illustrations are also created to record history. These historical documents are called **primary source materials**.

At first, some things written in earlier times may seem difficult to understand. Language changes over the years, and the objects and activities described might be unfamiliar. Also, spellings were sometimes different. Below is a model which describes how we help with these challenges.

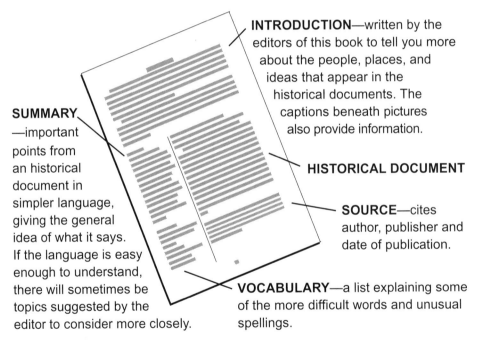

INTRODUCTION—written by the editors of this book to tell you more about the people, places, and ideas that appear in the historical documents. The captions beneath pictures also provide information.

SUMMARY—important points from an historical document in simpler language, giving the general idea of what it says. If the language is easy enough to understand, there will sometimes be topics suggested by the editor to consider more closely.

HISTORICAL DOCUMENT

SOURCE—cites author, publisher and date of publication.

VOCABULARY—a list explaining some of the more difficult words and unusual spellings.

In these historical documents, you may see three periods (…) called an ellipsis. It means that the editor has left out some words or sentences. You may see some words in brackets, such as [and]. These are words the editor has added to make the meaning clearer. When you use a document in a paper you're writing, you should include any ellipses and brackets it contains, just as you see them here. Be sure to give complete information about the author, title, and publisher of anything that was written by someone other than you.

Introduction: Enslaving Others
by Pat Perrin

A **slave** is a person who is owned by another person—and who must serve his or her owner. **Slavery** is the practice of using slaves. To **enslave** others is to force them to be slaves.

Slavery began far back in human history, before records were kept. Europeans, Arabs, Asians, Africans, and Native Americans all enslaved others. When ancient Greece was at its height, Athens had more than twice as many slaves as free citizens.

In civilizations that kept slaves, explanations were offered to show that slavery was both natural and moral. All of these arguments said that the enslaved people were inferior, and that slavery was their natural state. Christians defended slavery with passages from the Bible.

In those earlier times, most slaves were captives taken in war. Some were citizens being punished. Most worked as personal servants, and they were usually not of a different race from their owners.

In 1441, a Portuguese ship captain first captured some Africans and sold them in Europe. At that time, the market for slaves was small, because there weren't many uses for them. Then the New World was discovered, and the market suddenly expanded. Slaves were needed for producing sugar (and a bit later, tobacco) that was much desired in Europe.

The New World's natives proved to be poor slaves. For one thing, they could escape and return home. The best source of large numbers of slaves who couldn't easily get away was Africa. So **commercial slavery** on a large scale began for the first time in history.

Europeans made familiar arguments defending slavery. The Africans were heathens (not believers in a recognized religion). They had no civilization of their own. They would actually benefit from enslavement by more civilized, Christian people.

In fact, there had been several great empires in Africa, parts of which remained in the 15th century. Many village-states had stable governments and economies. They produced a variety of crops, textiles, and metal goods. In Benin, for example, Africans had been making beautiful metal sculptures for hundreds of years.

However, African culture was different from that in Europe, and was not understood or respected by the Europeans. It was convenient for them to think of Africans as savages, cursed by God, and only suitable for slavery.

The Triangle of Trade

In the 17th century, foreign trade was very profitable for the British. In 1672, the king created the Royal African Company of England "for the buying, selling, bartering and exchanging of, for, or with any Gold, Silver, Negroes, Slaves, goods, wares and merchandizes...."

Ships left England loaded with trade goods. On the west coast of Africa, they exchanged their cargo for human beings. They took the slaves to the West Indies or the American colonies and traded them for sugar and other products. They took those goods to England. Every leg of the triangle was profitable.

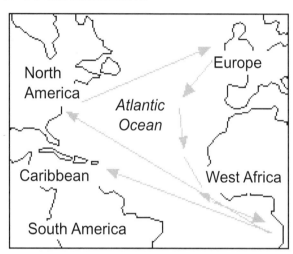

In 1750, the British king signed a new act to increase the triangular trade.

Summary:

The trade with Africa is very good for Britain. It is necessary to supply the Colonies with enough Negroes at reasonable prices. Therefore, his Majesty's subjects may trade in any west African port without limitations.

Vocabulary:

advantageous = profitable; beneficial

traffick (traffic) = exchange goods

whereas = since

Whereas the Trade to and from Africa is very advantageous to Great Britain, and necessary for the supplying the Plantations and Colonies... with a sufficient Number of Negroes at reasonable Rates;... Therefore be it enacted.... That it shall and may be lawful for all his Majesty's Subjects to trade and traffick to and from any Port or Place in Africa, [on the west coast]...without any Restraint whatsoever....

Source: An Act for Extending and Improving the Trade to Africa, 1750. Charter of the Royal African Company. Found in Elizabeth Donnan, *Documents Illustrative of the History of the Slave Trade to America—Volume I—1441–1700.* New York: Octagon Books, Inc., p. 473, originally published in 1930.

Placing an Order

Many in the colonies were eager to have ready labor, and arrangements for the delivery of Africans were made like any other goods. In 1683, Virginia planter and merchant William Fitzhugh wrote to a shipper in Portsmouth, New Hampshire.

Mr. Jackson: As to your proposal about the bringing in Negroes next fall, I have this to offer and you may communicate the same to your owners and Employers, that I will deal with them for so many as shall amount to 50,000 lbs of Tob'o and cask which will be about 20 hhds, under the condition and at these ages and prices following, to say—to give 3000 lbs Tob'o for every Negro boy or girl, that shall be between the age of Seven and Eleven years old; to give 4000 lbs Tob'o for every youth or girl that shall be between the age of 11 to 15 and to give 5000 lbs Tob'o for every young man or woman that shall be above 15 years of age and not exceed 24, the said Negroes to be delivered at my landing some time in September next, and I to have notice whether they will so agree some time in August next....

Source: Elizabeth Donnan, *Documents Illustrative of the History of the Slave Trade to America - Volume IV - The Border Colonies and the Southern Colonies.* New York: Octagon Books, Inc., 1965, p. 57, originally published in 1935.

Summary:

As for your plans to bring in Negroes next fall, here's my offer. I will take as many as amount to 50,000 lbs of tobacco and about 20 barrels of rum. I'll give 3000 lbs of tobacco for every Negro boy or girl between 7 and 11 years old; 4000 lbs for every one between 11 and 15, and 5000 lbs for every one between 15 and 24. They must be delivered at my dock next September, and I must be notified in August whether the order will be filled.

Vocabulary:

cask, hhds (hogsheads) = large containers or barrels of rum

Tob'o = tobacco

Horrors of the Middle Passage

Many African kings had slaves—usually captives from tribal wars. When the kings discovered the profits to be made, some of them began to capture and sell members of other tribes. Slavery became a commercial activity for them, as well as for the Europeans.

The trip from Africa to the New World was called the Middle Passage— and it was a journey filled with horror. The Europeans packed as many captives as they could onto their ships. They chained them together, with little room to move.

Enslaved Africans on the deck of the bark Wildfire, *Key West, April 30, 1860.* (Wood engraving, found at Digital Schomburg Images of 19th Century African Americans, originally printed in *Harpers' Weekly*, June 2, 1860.)

Diseases such as smallpox and dysentery often broke out on the slave ships. Captives who had contagious diseases were thrown overboard to keep the disease from spreading. The food was poor, and sometimes the captives went on hunger strikes. Others committed suicide if they got the opportunity. All of this added up to many, many deaths among the captives. *(See page 51)*

At least some African lives were lost on most voyages. A list made in the late 18th century showed that of 7,904 captives, 2,053 lives were lost in the crossing (26 percent). A 1784 British estimate was 12.4 percent.

Source: Figures are from John Hope Franklin, *An Illustrated History of Black Americans.* New York: Time-Life Books, 1970, p. 16.

A diary kept by Richard Drake described some of the horrors of the Middle Passage.

I am growing sicker every day of this business of buying and selling human beings for beasts of burden... On the eighth day [out at sea] I took my round of the half deck, holding a camphor bag in my teeth; for the stench was hideous. The sick and dying were chained together. I saw pregnant women give birth to babies whilst chained to corpses, which our drunken overseers had not removed. The blacks were literally jammed between decks as if in a coffin, and a coffin that dreadful hold became to nearly one half of our cargo before we reached [port].

Source: *The Journal of Richard Drake.* Found in James Pope-Hennesey, *Sins of the Fathers,* New York: Alfred A. Knopf, 1968, p 4.

Commentary:
Not all European sailors and traders were able to harden themselves to the horrors they witnessed.

Vocabulary:
camphor = a strong-smelling medicine
hold = lower area in a ship for storing cargo
literally = actually; without exaggeration
overseer = supervisor
stench = stink
whilst = while

A Child Witness

J.B. Romaigne was 12 years old when he sailed as a passenger on the French ship *Le Rodeur*. It was 1819, and although the British dominated the slave trade, other countries also took part in it. J.B. Romaigne's journey took him from France to Africa, and then to the West Indies with a cargo of slaves. He wrote down what he saw in his diary.

Summary:

Today a black captive suddenly knocked down a sailor and tried to jump overboard. Another sailor caught him and slashed the tendon behind the slave's knee. The Captain knocked the sailor down, because the slave had been the best of the bunch. They dropped the black man into the sea because now he was crippled. I saw that he kept swimming even after he began to sink. The red trail was headed for the shore, but then it stopped. It grew wider and faded away.

Vocabulary:

cutlass = short sword with a curved blade

hamstrung = crippled by cutting the tendon behind the knee

hold = lower area in a ship for storing cargo

oath = curse

passion = anger

…Today, one of the blacks whom they were forcing into the hold, suddenly knocked down a sailor and attempted to leap overboard. He was caught, however, by the leg by another of the crew, and the sailor, rising up in a passion, hamstrung him with a cutlass. The Captain, seeing this, knocked the butcher flat upon the deck…. 'I will teach you to keep your temper,' said he, with an oath. 'He was the best slave in the lot.' I ran…and looked…for they had dropped the black into the sea when they saw that he was useless. He continued to swim, even after he had sunk under water, for I saw the red track extending shoreward; but by and by, it stopped, widened, faded, and I saw it no more.

Source: *Diary of J.B. Romaigne*. Found in the Introduction by Ernest Pentecost to George Francis Dow, *Slave Ships and Slaving*. Salem, Massachusetts: Marine Research Society, 1927, pp. xxviii–xxxv.

A Child Kidnapped

Children as well as adults were taken from Africa to serve as slaves. (Remember that William Fitzhugh placed an order for boys and girls between 7–11, 11–15, and over 15.) Olaudah Equiano was 11 years old in 1756 when he was kidnapped and taken to America. He later wrote about his experiences on board the ship.

When I was carried on board I was immediately handled, and tossed up, to see if I were sound, by some of the crew.… I was soon put down under the decks, and there I became so sick that I was not able to eat. Two of the white men offered me eatables; and, on my refusing to eat, one of them held me fast while the other flogged me severely. The closeness of the place, added to the number in the ship, almost suffocated us. The shrieks of the women, and the groans of the dying rendered the whole a scene of horror almost inconceivable. One day two of my wearied countrymen who were chained together, preferring death to such a life of misery …jumped into the sea [and] were drowned.

Source: Olaudah Equiano (renamed Gustaves Vassa), *The Interesting Narrative of the Life of Olaudah Equiano or Gustaves Vassa, The African.* New York, 1791. Found in John Hope Franklin, *An Illustrated History of Black Americans,* New York: Time-Life Books, 1970, p. 19.

Summary:
When I was taken on board I was grabbed by some of the crew and checked to see if I was in good condition. I was put below deck, and got so sick I couldn't eat. Two white men offered me food. When I refused, one held me while the other whipped me hard. The small, tight place and the number of people almost suffocated us. The screams of the women and groans of the dying were horrible beyond belief. One day two of my tired countrymen, who were chained together, chose death over a life of misery. They jumped into the sea and were drowned.

Vocabulary:
eatables = food
flogged = whipped
rendered = made; created
shrieks = screams

Olaudah Equiano was taken to Barbados to be sold. He later wrote, "I was conducted immediately to the merchant's yard, where we were all pent up together like so many sheep in a fold.... I remember...there were several brothers, who in the sale were sold in different lots...."

Source: Olaudah Equiano (renamed Gustaves Vassa), *The Interesting Narrative of the Life of Olaudah Equiano or Gustaves Vassa, The African.* New York, 1791.

Olaudah Equiano was re-named Gustavus Vassa by one of his owners. He later earned his freedom, and became a successful civil servant and author. He even traveled on the seas again—as a free man.

Buying, Selling, and Trading People

In 1619, twenty African slaves were brought to Jamestown. They were the first slaves in the English colonies in America. At that time, they were thought of like white indentured servants, who could theoretically serve their time and earn their freedom. But as the plantation system grew in the South, permanent slaves were in great demand. Millions of captive Africans were brought to the New World. John Hope Franklin quotes estimates that "900,000 were imported in the 16th Century; 2.75 million in the 17th, seven million in the 18th, and four million in the 19th."

Source: John Hope Franklin, *An Illustrated History of Black Americans.* New York: Time-Life Books, 1970, p. 19.

For nearly 250 years, people were bought and sold in America. The slaves could be resold or traded over and over again. They could even be rented out to others who needed workers. And free black people were always at risk too.

Solomon Northrup was a free man from New York. When he went to Washington, D.C., in 1841, Northrup was kidnapped and sold into slavery. He later described a sale held by a man named Freeman.

[A planter from Baton Rouge] purchased Randall.... Eliza [Randall's mother] was crying aloud, and wringing her hands. She besought the man not to buy him, unless he also bought herself and Emily [her daughter]. She promised, in that case, to be the most faithful slave that ever lived. The man answered that he could not afford it, and then Eliza burst into a paroxysm of grief, weeping plaintively. Freeman turned round to her, savagely, with his whip in his up-lifted hand, ordering her to stop her noise, or he would flog her. Eliza kept on begging and beseeching them, most piteously, not to separate the three. But it was of no avail. The bargain was agreed upon, and Randall must go alone. Then Eliza ran to him; embraced him passionately; kissed him again and again; told him to remember her—all the while her tears falling in the boy's face like rain....

"Don't cry, mama. I will be a good boy. Don't cry," said Randall, looking back as they passed out the door.

Source: John Hope Franklin, *An Illustrated History of Black Americans*. New York: Time-Life Books, 1970, pp. 22-3.

Summary:

A farmer bought Randall. His mother, Eliza, was crying. She begged the man not to buy Randall unless he also bought her and her daughter Emily. The man said he couldn't afford it. Eliza burst into a wail of grief, and Freeman threatened to whip her if she didn't stop her noise. She begged, but it was no use. Randall was sold and must go alone. Eliza hugged and kissed him again and again, sobbing all the while.

As they left, Randall told his mama not to cry. "I will be a good boy," he said.

Vocabulary:

beseeching = begging
besought = begged
flog = whip
paroxysm = sudden
   outburst
passionately = with great
   feeling
piteously = pitifully
plaintively = sorrowfully
to no avail = no use

Poster of a Raffle for a horse and a slave girl. (Courtesy of Culver Pictures)

Slaves were considered property, like animals. This poster advertises the raffle of a horse and a woman—at a dollar each for chances. John Hope Franklin notes that "a slave woman named Sarah takes second billing to a trotting horse names Star."

Source: John Hope Franklin, *An Illustrated History of Black Americans.* New York: Time-Life Books, 1970, p. 20.

Opinions and Rationalizations

A rationalization is a reason you give for your behavior that makes you feel good, but is incorrect or dishonest. Many people used a variety of rationalizations for slavery. Others tried to think seriously and intelligently about the questions it raised. For example, were the Africans equal in ability to Europeans? And whether or not they were equal, did they deserve freedom?

Some simply believed that, for good or for evil, slavery was necessary.

In 1757, Reverend Peter Fontaine wrote to his brother about the excuses that were so easily made for having slaves.

Dear Brother Moses: …Like Adam we are all apt to shift off the blame from ourselves and lay it upon others.… The negroes are enslaved by the negroes themselves before they are purchased by the masters of the ships who bring them here. It is to be sure at our choice whether we buy them or not, so this then is our crime, folly, or whatever you will please to call it…[but] to live in Virginia without slaves is morally impossible. Before…[unless you could] cut wood, to go to mill, to work at the hoe, etc. you must starve, or board in some family where they [cheat strangers]. This of course draws us all into the original sin and curse of the country of purchasing slaves.…

Source: Elizabeth Donnan, *Documents Illustrative of the History of the Slave Trade to America,* Volume IV. New York: Octagon Books, 1965, pp. 142-3.

Commentary:
Fontaine suggests that slavery may be a crime, but that people in Virginia must have them—because without them, life is just too difficult for white people.

"Folly" now means "foolishness." But it also used to mean "evil" or "criminally foolish."

"Morally impossible" is probably used in the sense of "almost certainly impossible."

In the complete letter, Fontaine goes on to say that a slave for life only costs a little more than one would pay a free laborer for a year's work.

The Quakers Oppose Slavery

Members of the Society of Friends, often called Quakers, couldn't easily rationalize slavery. They believed that every human being contained a spark of God.

When Quaker John Woolman was a young shop assistant, he was told to write a bill of sale for a slave. He did so, but felt that he had failed his Christian beliefs. Next time, Woolman asked to be released from writing such a bill of sale—and was.

Some American Quakers did own slaves, though not after the early 1800s. Woolman and many others felt it was their duty to gently convince other people of slavery's evils. Woolman's journal recounts his many conversations on the subject. For example, some people argued that life in Africa was terrible. So, they said, taking Negroes as slaves was doing them a favor.

Summary:

I replied that if concern for Africans was our real reason for buying them, those feelings would make us treat them kindly. Like strangers rescued from suffering, they would live happily among us. But while we show by our actions that we buy them for our own benefit, to say they're unhappy in Africa is not a good argument in our favor.

Vocabulary:
affliction = state of
    suffering
compassion = concern
incite = provoke; urge on
manifest = show
motive = reason for action

To which I then replied, if Compassion on the Africans…were the real Motive of our purchasing them, that Spirit of Tenderness…would incite us to use them kindly, that, as Strangers brought out of Affliction, their Lives might be happy among us.… But while we manifest, by our conduct, that our Views in purchasing them are to advance ourselves…to say they live unhappy in Africa, is far from being an Argument in our Favour.

Source: John Woolman, *The Journal and Other Writings,* intro. Vida D. Scudder, London: J. M. Dent, 1910, pp. 26-7.

Benjamin Franklin

Although Benjamin Franklin once owned slaves himself, he came to disapprove of slavery. What worried Franklin most was the effect that slavery had on their white owners and on the country as a whole. In the 1750s, he wrote an essay about the problems he foresaw.

The Whites who have Slaves, not laboring, are enfeebled…the Slaves being work'd too hard and ill fed, their Constitutions are broken, and the Deaths among them are more than the Births; so that a continual Supply is needed from Africa. The…white Children become proud, disgusted with Labour, and being educated in Idleness, are rendered unfit to get a Living by Industry.

Source: Benjamin Franklin, *Observations concerning the Increase of Mankind, Peopling of Countries, &c.* Found in Nathaniel Weyl and William Marina, *American Statesmen On Slavery and the Negro,* New Rochelle, New York: Arlington House, 1971, p. 17.

Summary:
White people who have slaves don't work, and become weak. Slaves are worked too hard and fed too little. Their health is ruined. More die than are born, so more are always needed from Africa. White children become idle and unfit to earn a living.

Vocabulary:
constitution = physical condition
enfeebled = made weak
rendered = made

During the writing of the Constitution, Franklin took little interest in the arguments over slavery. He was completely focused on holding the new country together.

However, when Franklin was in his eighties, he was elected president of the Pennsylvania Society for Promoting the Abolition of Slavery and Relief of Free Negroes Unlawfully Held in Bondage and for Improving the Condition of the African Race. (Abolition means doing away with something.) Franklin's plans included education for children, apprenticeships for learning trades, and help in finding jobs. He also believed that freed slaves would need help in setting up rules of morality and conduct.

In 1790, Franklin signed a statement to Congress stating that "equal liberty is the birth-right of all men," and asking that the slaves be freed.

Source: Nathaniel Weyl and William Marina, *American Statesmen On Slavery and the Negro.* New Rochelle, New York: Arlington House, 1971, pp. 17, 22-3.

By the time America became an independent country, slavery was well established. Many of the country's founders owned slaves, and even those who didn't had to deal with the questions slavery raised. After all, the 1776 Declaration of Independence clearly says that "We hold these truths to be self-evident, that all men are created equal." It adds that all have rights which include "Life, Liberty and the pursuit of Happiness."

There were heated debates on slavery during the writing of the U. S. Constitution. But when it was ratified in 1788, it allowed the continuation of the slave trade for another 20 years.

Thomas Jefferson

Jefferson, who owned slaves, didn't consider the Africans equal to Europeans in intelligence or ability. But then, Jefferson didn't believe that people in general were equal in many ways. He thought that there was a natural aristocracy of virtue and talent among men. (An aristocracy is a group or class considered superior to others, by birth, wealth, or ability.)

Jefferson did believe that people were equally capable as far as morality was concerned. And he also insisted that people of all levels of ability deserved personal freedom. In his *Autobiography*, Jefferson expressed his thoughts on what lay ahead for the slaves.

Commentary:
Jefferson was sure that slaves would be freed. However, he didn't believe that white Americans and freed slaves should live in the same country.

Nothing is more certainly written in the book of fate than that these people are to be free; nor is it less certain that the two races, equally free, cannot live in the same government.

Source: Thomas Jefferson, *Autobiography*. Found in Nathaniel Weyl and William Marina, *American Statesmen On Slavery and the Negro*, New Rochelle, New York: Arlington House, 1971, p 71.

In 1790, Thomas Jefferson published his *Notes on the State of Virginia*. In "Query XIV," he discussed a bill to change Virginia's laws on slavery. However, nothing came of the idea in the Virginia legislature. His plan included freeing, educating, and deporting young Negroes.

They should continue with their parents to a certain age, then be brought up, at the public expence, to tillage, arts or sciences, according to their geniusses, till the females should be eighteen, and the males twenty-one years of age, when they should be colonized to such place as the circumstances of the time should render most proper, sending them out with arms, implements of household and of the handicraft arts, seeds, pairs of the useful domestic animals, &c. to declare them a free and independent people, and extend to them our alliance and protection, till they shall have acquired strength....

Source: Thomas Jefferson, *Notes on the State of Virginia, Query XIV.* Found in Nathaniel Weyl and William Marina, *American Statesmen On Slavery and the Negro,* New Rochelle, New York: Arlington House, 1971, p. 83.

Summary:
When old enough, they will be trained at public expense in farming, arts, or sciences, according to their talents. Females of 18 and males of 21 will be sent to the best place available, with weapons, tools, and animals. We will declare them independent and help them build up strength.

Vocabulary:
alliance = friendship
tillage = farming
geniusses (geniuses) = abilities

Jefferson and Benjamin Banneker

In spite of his beliefs about their intellectual abilities, Jefferson had a life-long interest in finding individual Negroes with talent.

Benjamin Banneker was a free Negro born in Maryland. Given books by a Quaker neighbor, Banneker showed an early talent for mathematics. Thomas Jefferson had him appointed to work with the French city planner L'Enfant. Banneker helped with surveying and laying out the new Capital at Washington. Banneker also published a series of almanacs, in which he disproved arguments about African inferiority.

Jefferson was delighted with the almanac, and with Banneker's achievements. He wrote to a friend that "I am happy to inform you that we now have in the United States a negro...who is a very respectable mathematician."

Source: Nathaniel Weyl and William Marina, *American Statesmen On Slavery and the Negro.* New Rochelle, New York: Arlington House, 1971, p. 91.

Lafayette and Washington

The young French Marquis de Lafayette was one of George Washington's favorite aides during the Revolutionary War. Two years after the war, Lafayette wrote Washington, proposing a plan to benefit "the black part of mankind."

Summary:

Let's buy a small farm together and free Negros to work there as tenants. Others might follow your example.

Vocabulary:

tenants = renters

render = make

Let us unite in purchasing a small estate, where we may try the experiment to free the Negroes, and use them only as tenants. Such an example as yours might render it a general practice....

Source: Nathaniel Weyl and William Marina, *American Statesmen On Slavery and the Negro.* New Rochelle, New York: Arlington House, 1971, p. 40.

George Washington

Washington disapproved of the African slave trade because of its cruelty. As a plantation owner, he saw no way out of slavery itself. He owned more than 100 slaves, and was apparently a kindly master. He neither broke up families nor sold older slaves who could no longer work. Later in life, Washington's disapproval of slavery grew stronger. He never felt financially stable enough to free his slaves, but his will set them free on Martha Washington's death.

Washington liked Lafayette's proposal, but gave his attention to holding the new nation together. He replied to Lafayette.

Summary:

To free the slaves all at once would produce problems. But it certainly ought to be done by degrees, and by law.

Vocabulary:

assuredly = definitely

by degrees = a little at a time

effected = carried out

To set the slaves afloat at once would, I really believe, be productive of much inconvenience and mischief; but by degrees it certainly might, and assuredly ought to be effected; and that too by legislative authority.

Source: Nathaniel Weyl and William Marina, *American Statesmen On Slavery and the Negro.* New Rochelle, New York: Arlington House, 1971, p. 40.

Defending Slavery

In both the North and South, many free but poor adults and children worked under horrible conditions. They had no protection against starvation. Some Americans argued that slavery actually took better care of the workers.

John C. Calhoun

John C. Calhoun of South Carolina served as a senator, as Vice-President of the United States under both John Quincy Adams and Andrew Jackson, and as secretary of state under John Tyler. As a senator, Calhoun was a powerful spokesman for slavery. He even managed to get a rule passed that barred Congress from discussing the issue.

Calhoun owned slaves, and was apparently fair with them. He didn't separate families or rent out his slaves to others. In the 1840s, Calhoun wrote:

The relation now existing in the slave-holding states between the two [races], is, instead of an evil, a positive good.… There never has yet existed a wealthy and civilized society in which one portion of the community did not, in point of fact, live on the labour of the other. Source: Nathaniel Weyl and William Marina, *American Statesmen On Slavery and the Negro.* New Rochelle, New York: Arlington House, 1971, p. 152.	**Commentary:** Calhoun argues that slavery is good because inequality is both traditional and necessary for civilization.

Those who thought that slavery could be defended usually held a certain view of humanity and of civilization. Calhoun stated it in in a political essay.

These great and dangerous errors have their origin in the prevalent opinion that all men are born free and equal;—than which nothing can be more unfounded and false. Source: John C. Calhoun, *A Disquisition on Government.* Found in Nathaniel Weyl and William Marina, *American Statesmen On Slavery and the Negro,* New Rochelle, New York: Arlington House, 1971, p. 149.	**Summary:** These huge mistakes begin with the belief that men are born free and equal. Nothing could be more wrong. **Vocabulary:** prevalent = widespread unfounded = groundless; not based on fact

The Rationalization of Comfort

William Cowper was an English poet in the last half of the 18th century. Like the Reverend Peter Fontaine, Cowper was well aware of British rationalizations that encouraged the slave trade to continue.

Commentary:
Cowper used satire to make fun of the selfish attitudes of those who traded in slaves. Satire is literature that reveals people's vices or stupidities by showing them to be ridiculous.

I own I am shocked at the purchase of
   slaves,
And fear those who buy them and sell them
   are knaves;
What I hear of their hardships, their tortures
   and groans,
Is almost enough to draw pity from stones.
I pity them greatly, but I must be mum,
For how could we do without sugar and
    rum?

Source: George Francis Dow, *Slave Ships and Slaving.* Salem, Massachusetts, 1927, 1st page of Chapter V.

Arguments about slavery in America went on—and on. Whenever new territory was added, there was debate about whether slavery would be legal there. In 1820, an agreement called The Missouri Compromise forbade the creation of more slave states north of Missouri's southern boundary. But in 1845, Texas was annexed, creating a huge new slave-holding state. Some Americans objected to the war with Mexico that began in 1846, because they believed that its true purpose was to add more slave-holding territory to the union.

But slavery continued. To many people—both in the North and the South—ending it seemed impossible. After all, it made a lot of money for a lot of people. In 1835, a New York merchant told a man who was against slavery, "The business of the North, as well as the South, has become adjusted to it. There are millions upon millions of dollars due from Southerners to the merchants and mechanics of this city alone. We cannot afford to let you and your associates succeed [in ending slavery]."

Source: John Hope Franklin, *An Illustrated History of Black Americans.* New York: Time-Life Books, 1970, p. 23.

Plantation workers in 1862, Edisto Island, South Carolina. (Courtesy of the New York Historical Society)

Slave Life

The enslaved Africans had to adjust to a lifetime as someone else's property. Some were treated better than others, but none had freedom.

I was young, and they had not treated me very badly; but I had seen older men treated worse than a horse or a hog ought to be treated. … My father being overseer, I was not used so badly as some even younger than myself, who were kicked, cuffed, and whipped very badly for little or nothing.…

I look upon slavery as the most disgusting system a man can live under.… Men who have never seen or felt slavery cannot realize it for the thing it is. If those who say that fugitives had better go back, were to go to the South and see slavery, they would never wish any slave to go back.

Source: James Adams, from Benjamin Drew, ed., *The Refugee: or Narratives of Fugitive Slaves in Canada Related by Themselves.* Boston, 1856.

Summary:

I was young, and my father was overseer, so I wasn't treated badly. I saw men treated worse than an animal should be. And younger ones were kicked, hit, and whipped for no good reason.

Slavery is disgusting. Those who have never been slaves cannot know how bad it is. If they saw it, the wouldn't think runaways should return.

Vocabulary:

cuffed = hit
fugitives = runaways
overseer = supervisor

Separating Families

One of the greatest hardships—and greatest terrors—for slaves was the loss of family members. Although a few slave-holders tried to keep families together, most sold people whenever it suited them. The owners made decisions according to what was convenient and profitable for them.

Thomas Hedgbeth

Thomas Hedgbeth was born free in Halifax, North Carolina, then moved to Indiana, and later to Canada. Hedgbeth wasn't a slave, but—like any other Negro—he was forbidden to learn to read and write.

In 1855, Boston educator and journalist Benjamin Drew collected and published interviews with Africans who had run away to Canada. Hedgbeth told Drew what he had seen in the South.

Summary:
I've seen families sold. I remember one near me that was sold after their master died. The father went to one owner, the mother and one child went to another. The other two children went another way. I saw the sale. The buyer examined the slaves' bodies to see if they were sound. I hated to see it. The oldest child was 10 or 11 years. It was hard for them, and they mourned and cried. I never heard a white seller ask that a family be sold together.

Vocabulary:
lamentations = expressions of grief

I have seen families put on the block and sold. … I remember a family about two miles from me,—a father and mother and three children. Their master died, and they were sold. The father went one way, the mother another, with one child, and the other two children another way. I saw the sale—I was there—I went to buy hogs. The purchaser examined the persons of the slaves to see if they were sound,—if they were "good niggers." I was used to such things, but it made me feel bad to see it. The oldest was about ten or eleven years. It was hard upon them to be separated—they made lamentations about it. I never heard a white man at a sale express a wish that a family might be sold together.

Source: Thomas Hedgbeth, from Benjamin Drew, ed., *The Refugee: or Narratives of Fugitive Slaves in Canada Related by Themselves.* Boston, 1856, pp. 276-80.

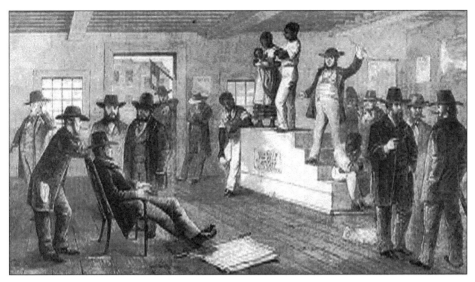

Slaves were auctioned off to the highest bidder at auctions like this one in Virginia. Families were often split up. (Schomberg Center– Photographs & Prints)

Harriet Jacobs

Although she was born a slave, Harriet Jacobs was taught to read and spell by the woman who owned her. Jacobs later wrote about her life.

I saw a mother lead seven children to the auction-block. She knew that some of them would be taken from her; but they took all. The children were sold to a slave-trader, and their mother was bought by a man in her own town. Before night her children were all far away. She begged the trader to tell her where he intended to take them; this he refused to do. How could he, when he knew he would sell them, one by one, wherever he could command the highest price? I met that mother in the street, and her wild, haggard face lives to-day in my mind. She wrung her hands in anguish, and exclaimed, "Gone! All gone! Why don't God kill me?"

Source: Harriet Jacobs, *Incidents in the Life of a Slave Girl*, published in 1860. Found in Digital Schomburg African American Women Writers of the 19th Century, on the New York Library website: http:lldiglib.nyol.org.

Summary:
I saw a mother and seven children auctioned off. All her children were sold to a slave-trader. The mother was sold to a man in town. The trader refused to tell her where the children were going. He couldn't, because he would sell them wherever he got the best price. I met her later, and she cried, "Why don't God kill me?"

Vocabulary:
anguish = mental pain
haggard = exhausted

Rented Out

On some farms, the owner worked slaves at home until the corn and cotton were harvested, then rented them out. The practice of leasing slaves to other people produced some of the greatest cruelties of all. Those who rented slave labor were interested in getting the most for their money. They had little interest in the well-being of the workers.

Harriet Jacobs saw the process in person.

Summary:

Slaves are hired on January 1st and go to new masters on the 2nd. They take their belongings and wait to hear what will happen. Any slave knows which master in the area is kind or cruel. It's easy to tell, because one who clothes and feeds slaves well is surrounded by people begging him to hire him. If a slave doesn't want to go with a new master, he's whipped or put in jail until he gives in and also promises not to run away.

Vocabulary:

alls = belongings
humane = kind
massa = master
thronged = surrounded by

Hiring-day at the south takes place on the 1st of January. On the 2d, the slaves are expected to go to their new masters…. They gather together their little alls, or more properly speaking, their little nothings, and wait anxiously for the dawning of day. At the appointed hour the grounds are thronged with men, women, and children, waiting, like criminals, to hear their doom pronounced. The slave is sure to know who is the most humane, or cruel master, within forty miles of him. It is easy to find out, on that day, who clothes and feeds his slaves well; for he is surrounded by a crowd, begging, "Please, massa, hire me this year. I will work very hard, massa." If a slave is unwilling to go with his new master, he is whipped, or locked up in jail, until he consents to go, and promises not to run away during the year.

Source: Harriet Jacobs, *Incidents in the Life of a Slave Girl*, published in 1860. Found in Digital Schomburg African American Women Writers of the 19th Century, on the New York Library website: http:lldiglib.nyol.org.

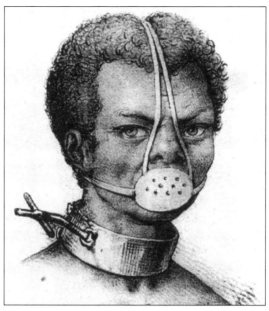

Slave with Iron Muzzle by Jacques Etienne Victor Arago. Equiano described a similar scene in his biography: "I had seen a black woman slave as I came through the house, who was cooking the dinner, and the poor creature was cruelly loaded with various kinds of iron machines; she had one particularly on her head, which locked her mouth so fast that she could scarcely speak, and could not eat or drink. I [was] much astonished and shocked at this contrivance, which I afterwards learned was called the iron muzzle." — Olaudah Equiano

if he runs away...

Should he chance to change his mind, thinking it justifiable to violate an extorted promise, woe unto him if he is caught! The whip is used till the blood flows at his feet; and his stiffened limbs are put in chains, to be dragged in the field for days and days! If he lives until the next year, perhaps the same man will hire him again, without even giving him an opportunity of going to the hiring-ground.

Source: Harriet Jacobs, *Incidents in the Life of a Slave Girl,* published in 1860. Found in Digital Schomburg African American Women Writers of the 19th Century, on the New York Library website: http:lldiglib.nyol.org.

Summary:

If the slave runs away —thinking he doesn't have to keep a forced promise—it's terrible for him if he's caught. He's whipped until blood flows. He drags chains through the fields for days. If he lives, the same man might hire him again next year.

Vocabulary:

extorted = obtained by force or intimidation
woe = misfortune

Decent Treatment Doesn't Equal Freedom

Even slaves who were not mistreated wanted to be free. Sometimes owners were amazed when well-treated slaves ran away or asked to buy their freedom.

James Christian

James Christian gained a little education when he went to the college of William and Mary to wait on his young master. Christian was inherited by the wife of President Tyler, and wound up working in the White House. Christian made no complaints about the way he was treated.

Commentary:
Some slaves who escaped or were set free had a very hard time making a living. One reason was that, in the South, it was illegal to teach them how to read or write.

"I have always been treated well; if I only have half as good times in the North as I have had in the South, I shall be perfectly satisfied. Any time I desired spending money, five or ten dollars were no object."

Source: William Still, *The Underground Rail Road.* Philadelphia, 1872, pp. 69-70. Found in William Loren Katz, *Eyewitness: A Living Documentary of the African American Contribution to American History,* New York: Simon and Schuster, 1995 pp. 130-1.

However, because he was a slave, Christian could not marry the free African American woman that he loved. Christian ran away from the White House, and was later interviewed in Philadelphia.

Occasionally slaves had the Sabbath day off, to socialize, dance, sing, and play. They also attended services and did their domestic chores.

Slavery wasn't limited to the South. There were also some slaves held in Northern states. Slaves in the North were likely house servants, shop helpers, or workers in some trade. The slave pictured here was a coachman.

Henry Blue

A few slaves were allowed to save money and to purchase their own freedom. Henry Blue explained why he wanted to.

I learned the trade of a blacksmith in Kentucky. I should have been perfectly miserable to have had to work all my life for another man for nothing. As soon as I [was old enough] I felt determined that I would not be a slave all my days. My master was a kind and honorable man; purchased no slaves himself: what he had, came by marriage. He used to say it was wrong to hold slaves, and a good many who hold them say the same. It's a habit—they mean, they say, to set them free at such a time, or such a time,— by and by they die, and the children hold on to the slaves.

Source: Benjamin Drew, ed., *The Refugee: or Narratives of Fugitive Slaves in Canada Related by Themselves.* Boston, 1856, p. 276.

Commentary:
Henry Blue understood very well why some people had slaves. Once they owned them, even well-meaning owners found it very hard to let them go.

Spirituals

Spirituals are a type of religious songs originally composed and sung by African American slaves. Frederick Douglass was a slave who learned to read and write—and who later became a famous speaker and author.

Summary:

Spirituals were the prayer and complaint of souls in terrible pain. Every sound testified against slavery and prayed for freedom. The songs of a slave show the sorrows of his heart. The songs help, but only like tears help an aching heart.

Vocabulary:

anguish = terrible pain; torment

relieved = freed from pain

represent = stand for; present

testimony = evidence; proof

Frederick Douglass

Spirituals breathed the prayer and complaint of souls boiling over with the bitterest anguish. Every tone was a testimony against slavery, and a prayer to God for deliverance from chains.... The songs of the slave represent the sorrows of his heart; and he is relieved by them, only as an aching heart is relieved by its tears.

Source: Frederick Douglass, *Narrative of the Life of Frederick Douglass, An American Slave, Written by Himself.* Boston: 1845; New York: Doubleday & Co., 1963.

Nobody Knows De Trouble I See

Chorus
Nobody knows de trouble I see,
Nobody knows but Jesus;
Nobody knows de trouble I see,
Glory hallelujah!

Sometimes I'm up, sometimes I'm down,
Oh, yes, Lord;
Sometimes I'm almost to de groun',
Oh, yes, Lord.
Altho' you see me goin' 'long so,
Oh, yes, Lord;
I have my trials here below,
Oh, yes, Lord.

Chorus
Oh, nobody knows de trouble I see,
Nobody knows but Jesus;
Nobody knows de trouble I see,
Glory hallelujah!

Looking Back

Between 1934 and 1941, some former slaves were interviewed by the Federal Writer's Project. It was part of the Works Progress Administration (WPA) efforts to provide employment during America's Great Depression.

Mary Reynolds

Slavery was the worst days that was ever seed in the world. They was things past tellin,' but I got the scars on my old body to show to this day. I seed worse than what happened to me ...

Mary Ferguson

'Bout de middle of de evening,' up rid my young marster on his hoss, an' up driv' two strange white mens in a buggy. Dey hitch deir hosses and come in de house, which skeered me. Den, one o' de strangers said, "Git yo' clothes, Mary. We has bought yo' from Mr. Shorter." I c'menced crying and beggin' Mr. Shorter not to let 'em take me away. But he said "Yes, Mary, I has sole yer, an' yer must go wid 'em.

Den, dose strange mens, whose names I ain't never knowed, tuk me an' put me in de buggy and driv' off wid me, me hollering at de top o' my voice an' callin' my ma....

I ain't never seed nor heard tell o' my ma an' paw, an' brothers, an' sisters, from dat day to dis.

Katie Rowe

Old Man Saunders was de hardest overseer of anybody. He would git mad and give a whipping some time, and de slave wouldn't even know what it was about....

Source: *Bullwhip Days*. New York: Mellon, Weidenfeld, & Nicholson, 1988, pp. 18-9, 28-32, and 293.

Commentary:

The writers who interviewed the former slaves tried to reproduce their dialect. Dialect is the way a language is spoken by a particular group of people, or in a particular area. Sometimes writers use odd spellings and punctuation to give readers an idea of how a dialect sounds. Written dialect can be easier to understand if you read it aloud.

Anti-Slavery Acts and Words

Of course, not everyone accepted slavery. Some people tried to change things. David Walker was an educated free black man. He traveled through the South, and saw what slavery was like.

Walker had a store on the Boston waterfront, where he sold used clothing. In 1829, he wrote an Appeal, telling slaves to revolt. He hid copies of it in the pockets of the clothes he sold. Walker knew that some copies would reach used-clothes dealers in Southern ports. He also gave copies of the Appeal to black sailors who could pass them around in the South.

David Walker's Appeal caused great alarm in the Southern states. Laws were quickly passed against such literature. New laws also made it illegal for slaves to learn to read and write.

Most people rejected Walker's call for violence. But his work did attract attention to slavery's evils. Following is some of the advice he gave.

Summary:
Never try to get free until you see that it's possible. When that time comes, and you move, don't be afraid.

If you start, then kill or be killed. Wouldn't you rather be killed than be a slave to a tyrant who kills all your family? There's no harm in killing a man who's trying to kill you.

Vocabulary:
be dismayed = lose
   courage
commence = begin
oppressors = ones who
   rule by force
tyrant = cruel ruler

David Walker's Appeal

'Never make an attempt to gain our freedom or natural right, from under our cruel oppressors and murderers, until you see your way clear —when that hour arrives and you move, be not afraid or dismayed....

If you commence kill or be killed. Now, I ask you, had you not rather be killed than to be a slave to a tyrant, who takes the life of your mother, wife and dear little children? ...believe this, that it is no more harm for you to kill a man, who is trying to kill you, than it is for you to take a drink of water when thirsty....'

(continued on next page)

Walker addressed part of his appeal to white Americans.

But remember, Americans, [how] miserable, wretched, degraded and abject as you have made us…to support you and your families…. You want slaves, and want us for your slaves!!! My colour will yet, root some of you out of the very face of the earth!!!!!!'

Summary:
Remember how miserable you have made us to support youself and your families. You want us for slaves! We'll wipe some of you off the earth!

Vocabulary:
abject = low
degraded = disgraced
wretched = in miserable
  condition

Source: Courtesy of the Museum of Afro American History, Boston, MA, from Margaret A. Drew and William S. Parsons, *The African Meeting House in Boston – A Sourcebook,* The Museum of Afro American History, 1990.

Walker was warned that his life was in danger, but he refused to flee to Canada. One day, his body was found near his shop. Many people felt sure he had been poisoned.

Nat Turner was captured and shot.

Nat Turner's Revolt

In 1831, a slave named Nat Turner led a revolt in Virginia. He and his men killed about 57 whites before the revolt was put down. Turner and some of his followers were captured and executed. *(See page 54)*

John Brown holds hostages at bay with a rifle. (Courtesy of the Western Reserve Historical Society)

John Brown's Raid

In 1859, a man from Kansas led a group of black and white men in an uprising to end slavery. To get weapons, they raided the federal arsenal at Harper's Ferry, Virginia (now West Virginia). They got inside the arsenal, but were soon surrounded by local and federal troops. Ten of Brown's men were killed in the battle. John Brown and two of his men were tried and hanged.

John A. Copeland, Jr.

One of those sentenced to hang was a Negro born of free parents in North Carolina. John Copeland wrote to his parents from prison.

Commentary:
Copeland thought of the raid as a revolution—just like the one that freed America from England.

Remember that if I must die I die in trying to liberate a few of my poor and oppressed people. ...I am not terrified by the gallows, which I see staring me in the face, and upon which I am soon to stand and suffer death for what George Washington was made a hero for doing....

Source: John Hope Franklin, *An Illustrated History of Black Americans.* New York: Time-Life Books, 1970, p. 44.

Abolitionists

People who wanted to abolish slavery were called abolitionists. (To abolish something is to do away with it.) In the 18th and early 19th centuries, abolitionists in Britain and France protested slavery and the African slave trade. Abolitionists soon organized in the United States too. By the 1830s, they were demanding an immediate end to slavery. These groups included blacks and women, as well as white males. They published newspapers, held rallies, gave speeches, passed out anti-slavery literature, and sent petitions to state governments. They also founded libraries and schools.

David Walker was an active Abolitionist. In addition to his Appeal, Walker wrote for the black-owned newspaper, *Freedom's Journal.* In 1831, the year after Walker's death, a white Bostonian began publishing his own anti-slavery newspaper.

William Lloyd Garrison

Garrison wrote that he admired David Walker's Appeal. Garrison's newspaper, *The Liberator*, influenced many others to support abolition and to help slaves who escaped. In it, Garrison published his own Manifesto. *(See page 55)*

Assenting to the "self-evident truth" maintained in the American Declaration of Independence, "that all men are created equal, and endowed by their creator with certain inalienable rights—among which are life, liberty and the pursuit of happiness," I shall strenuously contend for the immediate enfranchisement of our slave population....

Source: William Lloyd Garrison, "Manifesto," *The Liberator*, Jan. 1, 1831.

Summary:
In agreement with the Declaration of Independence, I shall work for the immediate freeing of slaves.

Vocabulary:
assenting = agreeing
contend = struggle
endowed = provided
enfranchisement = freedom; citizenship
inalienable = that cannot be taken away
maintained = declared
self-evident = obvious
strenuously = vigorously

Uncle Tom's Cabin

A minister's daughter, a minister's wife, and a former schoolteacher, Harriet Beecher Stowe first came in touch with runaway slaves in Cincinnati. She learned about slavery and later visited the Southern states to see it for herself. She was deeply touched by reading slave narratives, including the writings of Frederick Douglass.

In 1850, Stowe wrote an emotional novel about the horrors of slavery—*Uncle Tom's Cabin; or, Life Among the Lowly.* It was first published as a serial in the *National Era,* an antislavery paper. The story became incredibly popular, and convinced many readers to join the anti-slavery movement. Stowe wrote about the harsh treatment of slaves and the separation of families.

Summary:

It was a clear, calm evening when the boat stopped at Louisville. The woman put her child in a cradle-like space and went to the rail. She hoped to see her husband.

When she came back, her child was gone. The trader told her the baby had been sold.

Vocabulary:

bewilderment = confusion
farst = first
intently = with great
   attention
thronged = crowded
tranquil = calm

It was a bright, tranquil evening when the boat stopped at the wharf at Louisville. The [slave] woman…hastily laid the child down in a little cradle formed by the hollow among the boxes…and then she sprung to the side of the boat, in hopes that, among the various hotel-waiters who thronged the wharf, she might see her husband. In this hope, she pressed forward to the front rails, and, stretching far over them, strained her eyes intently on the moving heads on the shore, and the crowd pressed in between her and the child.…

When the boat, creaking, and groaning, and puffing, had loosed from the wharf, and was beginning slowly to strain herself along, the woman returned to her old seat. The trader was sitting there,—the child was gone!

"Why, why,—where?" she began, in bewildered surprise.

"Lucy," said the trader, "Your child's gone; you may as well know it farst as last. You see, I know'd you couldn't take him down south; and I got a chance to sell him to a first-rate family, that'll raise him better than you can."

Source: Harriet Beecher Stowe, *Uncle Tom's Cabin.* New York: Penguin Books, 1981, pp. 205-12. Originally published in 1852.

Escape!

Many slaves ran away from captivity. Some went in search of lost family members who had been sold to other owners. Their owners often published reward notices in newspapers.

$25 Reward. —Ran away, a Negro man, named Cain. He was brought from Florida, and has a wife near Mariana, and probably will attempt to make his way there. (Macon, Georgia, *Messenger,* November 23, 1837.)

Ran away from the subscriber, Ben. He ran off without any known cause, and I suppose he is aiming to go to his wife, who was carried from the neighborhood last winter. (Richmond, Virginia, *Compiler,* September 8, 1837.)

Stop the Runaway!!!! —$25 Reward. Ran away from the Eagle Tavern, a Negro fellow named Nat. He is no doubt attempting to follow his wife, who was lately sold to a speculator named Redmond.... (Richmond, Virginia, *Enquirer*, February 20, 1838.)

$50 Reward. —Ran away from the subscriber, a Negro girl, named Maria. She is of a copper color, between 13 and 14 years of age—bare headed and bare footed. She is small of her age.... She stated she was going to see her mother at Maysville. (Lexington, Kentucky, *Observer and Reporter*, September 28, 1838.)

Source: Theodore Dwight Weld, *American Slavery As It Is: Testimony of a Thousand Witnesses* (New York, 1839), pp. 164-6. Found in William Loren Katz, *Eyewitness: A Living Documentary of the African American Contribution to American History.* New York: Simon and Schuster, 1995, pp. 116–7.

Commentary:
Some slaves escaped because they were desperate to see their loved ones again. Instead of leaving the South, they went to find family members who had been sold away. Since their owners could often guess exactly where they were going, many of these runaways were caught.

Vocabulary:
speculator = one who buys and sells, taking a risk on the chance of profit

Frederick Douglass on the Terrors of the Trip

Many slaves escaped with the hope of making their way to freedom in the North. But most of them knew very little about what they might face on such a journey. In his autobiography, Frederick Douglass described the terrors of those who longed for freedom.

Summary:

Our path was difficult, and we had no certainty of freedom even if we reached the end. We could be caught and returned—and treated ten times worse than before. It wasn't easy to overcome that fear. Freedom called us. But when we thought about the road, we often lost our courage. We saw death on every side—starvation, drowning, being torn apart by bloodhounds, bitten by scorpions, wild beasts, and snakes. Finally, after overcoming everything and reaching our goal, we would be caught and shot dead on the spot.

Vocabulary:

appalled = horrified; dismayed

assuming = taking

beset = surrounded; attacked

contending = struggling

craggy = rocky; rough

encountering = meeting

liability = likelihood; risk

Our path was beset with the greatest obstacles; and if we succeeded in gaining the end of it, our right to be free was yet questionable.... [We were faced with] the frightful liability of being returned to slavery—with the certainty of being treated tenfold worse than before—the thought was truly a horrible one, and one which it was not easy to overcome.... [But] away back in the dim distance, under the flickering light of the north star, behind some craggy hill or snow-covered mountain, stood a doubtful freedom...beckoning us to come and share its hospitality. ...but when we permitted ourselves to survey the road, we were frequently appalled. Upon either side we saw grim death, assuming the most horrid shapes. Now it was starvation, causing us to eat our own flesh;—now we were contending with the waves, and were drowned;—now we were overtaken, and torn to pieces by the fangs of the terrible bloodhound. We were stung by scorpions, chased by wild beasts, bitten by snakes, and finally, after having nearly reached the desired spot,—after swimming rivers, encountering wild beasts, sleeping in the woods, suffering hunger and nakedness,—we were overtaken by our pursuers, and...shot dead upon the spot.

Source: Frederick Douglass, *Narrative of the Life of Frederick Douglass, An American Slave, Written by Himself.* Boston: 1845; New York: Doubleday & Co., 1963, pp. 84-6.

The Fugitive Slave Acts

Douglass was right—slaves *were* in great danger of being caught and returned. Free Negroes could also be enslaved if someone claimed they had once been slaves. In both 1793 and 1850, under pressure from Southern states, Congress passed strict laws about runaway slaves. Those who escaped from one state to another could be captured and returned. Both laws denied the accused a jury trial. A judge could simply decide whether or not the accused had ever been a slave. Following are excerpts from the 1850 law.

…When a person held to service or labor in any State or Territory of the United States… [shall] escape into another State or Territory of the United States, the person or persons to whom such service or labor may be due, or his, her, or their agent or attorney,…may pursue and reclaim such fugitive person…[and may use] such reasonable force and restraint as may be necessary.… In no trial or hearing under this act shall the testimony of such alleged fugitive be admitted in evidence.…

Any person who shall knowingly and willingly obstruct, hinder, or prevent such claimant, his agent or attorney…from arresting such a fugitive…or shall rescue, or attempt to rescue, such fugitive…[shall] be subject to a fine not exceeding one thousand dollars, and imprisonment not exceeding six months.…

Source: Fugitive Slave Act, Thirty-first Congress, Sess. I Ch. 60 (1850).

Summary:

When a slave escapes from one state to another, the owner, or owner's agent or attorney, may chase and recapture the fugitive. They may use the necessary reasonable force. The testimony of the accused shall not be admitted as evidence.

Any person who prevents an arrest, or rescues or tries to help a fugitive, shall be fined up to $1000 and imprisoned for up to six months.…

Vocabulary:

alleged = supposed
claimant = one who makes
 a claim
exceeding = more than
fugitive = one who fled
hinder = interfere with
obstruct = block
restraint = means of
 holding
testimony = statement
 under oath

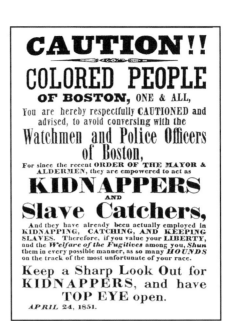

CAUTION!!
COLORED PEOPLE
OF BOSTON, ONE & ALL,
You are hereby respectfully **CAUTIONED** and advised, to avoid conversing with the
Watchmen and Police Officers of Boston,
For since the recent **ORDER OF THE MAYOR & ALDERMEN,** they are empowered to act as
KIDNAPPERS
AND
Slave Catchers,
And they have already been actually employed in **KIDNAPPING, CATCHING, AND KEEPING SLAVES.** Therefore, if you value your **LIBERTY,** and the *Welfare of the Fugitives* among you, *Shun* them in every possible manner, as so many *HOUNDS* on the track of the most unfortunate of your race.
Keep a Sharp Look Out for **KIDNAPPERS,** and have TOP EYE open.
APRIL 24, 1851.

The Fugitive Slave Acts were harsh and unreasonable. Because of them, more people than ever decided to fight slavery. Many Northern states passed new personal-liberty laws to block the slave acts. Posters were put out to warn the Negroes of the danger.

Henry David Thoreau

Thoreau was well-known as a speaker and writer. In 1854, he gave a speech against the Fugitive Slave Act of 1850. He made fun of the Massachusetts governor and of the military for enforcing that law. He called on citizens to pay more attention to what was going on.

Summary:
We don't realize what slavery is. If I suggested to Congress that we make people into sausages, they would think I was joking. Or they would think my idea was worse than anything Congress had done. But if they say that making a man into a sausage is worse than making him a slave, I will call him silly and stupid.

Vocabulary:
in earnest = seriously
incapacity = defect
proposition = plan

I think that we do not even yet realize what slavery is. If I were seriously to propose to Congress to make mankind into sausages, I have no doubt that most of the members would smile at my proposition, and if any believed me to be in earnest, they would think that I proposed something much worse than Congress had ever done. But if any of them will tell me that to make a man into a sausage would be much worse—would be any worse—than to make him into a slave—than it was to enact the Fugitive Slave Law, I will accuse him of foolishness, of intellectual incapacity....

Source: Henry David Thoreau, Address delivered at the Anti-Slavery Celebration, at Framingham, July 4, 1854. Found at website: http://www2.cybernex.net/-rlenat/slavery.html

Anti-slavery meeting on the Boston Common, 1851. Many abolitionists helped with the Underground Railroad. (Gleason's Pictorial Drawing Room Companion: May 1851, p. 4.)

The Underground Railroad

In spite of the dangers, enslaved African Americans escaped by the thousands. They headed north, to states where slavery wasn't legal. Because of the Fugitive Slave Acts, many went on to Canada. Most of them, by far, went on foot. They walked for hundreds of miles through dangerous territory, where they could be captured or killed at any moment.

How did they know where to go? Along the way, some people—both black and white—helped the fugitives. They signaled where it was safe to stop for the night. They provided hiding places. They gave advice on the safest route.

Some of these helpers lived along the way. Others were former slaves who came back and risked their own freedom to help others. These helpers put themselves in great danger. Some of them were caught and put in prison.

By the early 1800s, this secret system of routes, hiding places, and helpers was known as the Underground Railroad. As a code, the stopping places were called stations. The routes from one station to another were called lines. The helpers were conductors, and the fugitives were packages or freight. There aren't any complete records, but between 40,000 and 100,000 slaves reached freedom by way of the Underground Railroad.

Source: National Park Service Underground Railroad website: http://www.cr.nps.gov/nr/underground/.

Follow the Drinking Gourd

Information was often passed around in songs. A carpenter called Peg Leg Joe used to travel from farm to farm, teaching slaves the song "Follow the Drinking Gourd," to remind them how to find their way North. The Drinking Gourd was the Big Dipper, which includes the North star.

Commentary:

At mid-winter, the Sun rises in the southeast; it rises higher in the sky each day. Quail migrate south in the winter. This was a good time for slaves to leave. The old man is Peg Leg Joe.

The Tombigbee River leads northward from the Gulf of Mexico toward Tennessee. Drawings of a peg leg and a foot were left on dead trees to mark the way.

The Tennessee River flows northward across Tennessee and Kentucky. It meets the Ohio River over 800 miles north of Mobile, Alabama. Those who left southern Alabama or Mississippi in the winter would reach that point about a year later. That was the best time to cross, simply by walking across the ice.

Underground Railroad guides met fugitives on the northern bank and took them to safer areas.

When the Sun comes back
And the first quail calls
Follow the Drinking Gourd.
For the old man is a-waiting for to carry
   you to freedom
If you follow the Drinking Gourd.

The riverbank makes a very good road.
The dead trees will show you the way.
Left foot, peg foot, traveling on,
Follow the Drinking Gourd.

The river ends between two hills
Follow the Drinking Gourd.
There's another river on the other side
Follow the Drinking Gourd.

When the great big river meets the little river
Follow the Drinking Gourd.
For the old man is a-waiting for to carry
   you to freedom.

Source: The song and notes on its meaning were found on "Follow the Drinking Gourd," the Oklahoma Baptist University Planetarium website: http://www.okbu.edu/academics/natsci/planet/shows/gourd.htm

Harriet Tubman—Moses

Harriet Tubman escaped slavery, but went back into danger to lead others to freedom. As a conductor on the Underground Railroad, she helped more than 300 other slaves escape. People began to call her Moses, and rewards were offered for her capture. But Tubman was too smart and too determined to be taken into captivity again. She had strict rules for those she guided—anyone who gave out would be shot.

"Would you really do that?" she was asked. "Yes," she replied, "if he was weak enough to give out, he'd be weak enough to betray us all, and all who had helped us; and do you think I'd let so many die just for one coward man." "Did you ever have to shoot any one?" she was asked. "One time," she said, a man gave out the second night…he couldn't go any further; he'd rather go back and die, if he must." …Then she said, "I told the boys to get their guns ready, and shoot him. They'd have done it in a minute; but when he heard that, he jumped right up and went on as well as any body."

Source: *The Freedmen's Record*, Vol. 1, No. 3, Boston, March, 1865, pp. 34-8.

Summary:
Asked if she would really have shot someone, she said yes. She wouldn't risk everyone else for one coward. She said she nearly had to do it one time when a man insisted on going back. But when she told her boys to shoot, the man jumped up and went on as well as the others.

Hiding places were built into some houses and barns. A bed hid this short door that led to a small secret room. This Underground Railroad station is in the Levi Coffin house in Indiana. Coffin, a Quaker, helped so many runaways that he was sometimes called the "President" of the Underground Railroad.

Disguises

Some runaways disguised themselves cleverly. Men dressed as women and women as men, so they couldn't be easily identified. Before Anna Weems was 13, her whole family had been sold away. When she was 15, she became determined not to spend her life as a slave. Since men could travel more easily than women, Anna disguised herself as a male. She got away with the help of the Underground Railroad.

William and Ellen Craft were a married slave couple who longed to escape together. The lighter-skinned Ellen disguised herself as a white planter.

Ellen Craft in disguise

Since she was beardless, they wrapped up her face as though the planter had a toothache. To avoid having to register at hotels, they put one arm in a sling. The disguise also included a slight case of deafness, a limp, a cane, and tinted glasses. All of this made it important that the "young man" have his faithful servant always at his side.

Of course, that servant was William Craft. The couple made it to freedom together.

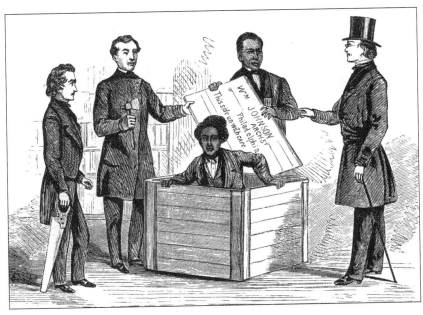

Henry "Box" Brown

One determined runaway shipped a 3' by 2' wooden crate north by train. Henry "Box" Brown was hidden inside. Unfortunately, the baggage handlers mostly ignored the message on the outside: "this side up with care." He was finally delivered alive to friends in Philadelphia, but he spent a dangerous amount of time traveling upside down.

In this dreadful position, I remained the space of an hour and a half, it seemed to me when I began to feel of my eyes and head, and found to my dismay, that my eyes were almost swollen out of their sockets, and the veins on my temple seemed ready to burst.... About half an hour afterwards, I attempted again to lift my hands to my face, but I found I was not able to move them. A cold sweat now covered me from head to foot.... One-half hour longer and my sufferings would have ended in [death].

Source: George Steams, *Narrative of Henry Box Brown by Himself.* Boston, 1849, pp. 60-2.

Summary:

I was upside down for what seemed about an hour and a half. My eyes were swollen and veins were standing out on my head. Half an hour later, I tried to lift my hands, but couldn't move them. I was in a cold sweat. Another half hour and I would have been dead.

Vocabulary:
dismay = alarm

Frederick Douglass Escapes

Some states required free Negroes to have identification papers. When he escaped at age 21, Frederick Douglass decided to use the papers of a sailor friend. But he knew they wouldn't pass a close inspection. *(See page 51)*

Summary:

The conductor asked for my papers. I said I never carried them at sea. I brought out the sailor's papers. Barely glancing at them, he took my fare and went on. If he had looked closely, he would have seen that it described a very different-looking person.

Vocabulary:

critical = dangerous

free papers = free Negro's identification papers

seaman's protection = a sailor's identification papers

[The conductor asked,] "I suppose you have your free papers?"

To which I answered: "No sir; I never carry my free papers to sea with me."

"But you have something to show that you are a freeman, haven't you?"

"Yes, sir," I answered; "I have a paper with the American Eagle on it, and that will carry me around the world."

With this I drew from my deep sailor's pocket my seaman's protection…. The merest glance at the paper satisfied him, and he took my fare and went on about his business…. Had the conductor looked closely at the paper, he could not have failed to discover that it called for a very different-looking person from my-self….

Source: Frederick Douglass, "My Escape from Slavery," *The Century Illustrated Magazine* 23, n.s. 1 (Nov. 1881), pp.125-31. Found on "Aboard the UnderGround Railroad," National Park Service Site: http://www.cr.nps.gov/nr/underground/

Ending Slavery

Most northern states outlawed slavery by 1804. But slavery was on the increase in the South, where labor was needed to grow great amounts of cotton. The slave trade—shipping slaves from Africa—was made illegal in England in 1807 and in the United States in 1808. However, slavery itself was still legal in the U. S., and African slaves were still smuggled in.

Lincoln and the Civil War

Abolitionists increased the pressure to end slavery. Southern slaveholders became defensive and angry. Their entire way of life depended upon the labor of slaves. For years, Southerners talked about secession—withdrawing from the United States and starting their own country.

When Abraham Lincoln was elected in 1860, he was considered an anti-slavery President. And he considered secession illegal.

During the next few months, South Carolina, Mississippi, Florida, Alabama, Georgia, and Louisiana all seceded from the union. They were later joined by Virginia, Arkansas, North Carolina, and Tennessee. In April of 1861, Confederate cannons opened fire on the Union military post at Fort Sumter, and the American Civil War had begun.

In 1862, Lincoln demanded that the rebel states return to the union. When no state returned, Lincoln issued the Emancipation Proclamation, declaring their slaves free. The paper didn't affect slaves in states on the Union side, and it was ignored in the South. However, from that time on, it was clear that the war was being fought for human freedom. The proclamation declared:

Emancipation Proclamation

That on the first day of January, in the year of our Lord one thousand eight hundred and sixty-three, all persons held as slaves within any State or designated part of a State, the people whereof shall then be in rebellion against the United States, shall be then, thenceforward, and forever free.

Source: Abraham Lincoln, The Emancipation Proclamation. Found in *An American Primer,* Daniel J. Boorstin, ec. New York: Penguin Books, 1966.

Summary:
On January 1, 1863, all people held as slaves within any state in rebellion against the United States, shall be then and forever free.

Vocabulary:
designated = selected
thenceforeward = from then on
whereof = of which

The Emancipation Proclamation also declared that Negroes "will be received into the armed service of the United States." Nearly 180,000 enlisted.

"Drummer" Jackson, 79th U. S. Colored Troops

The 13th Amendment

After the Civil War ended, the 13th Amendment to the Constitution was passed on December 18, 1865, officially and finally ending slavery in the United States.

Freedom and Reconstruction

When the war ended, many in the South were homeless and hungry. Cities, railways, roads, and bridges had been destroyed. Lincoln developed a plan to reorganize and rebuild. But the Reconstruction programs met with political opposition, and Lincoln didn't live to see if his plans could work. He was assassinated on April 14, 1865.

Many former slaves had to make a new life however they could. Some went north, others stayed where they were. Toby Jones became a pioneer.

Toby Jones

I worked for Massa 'bout four years after freedom, 'cause he forced me to, said he couldn't 'ford to let me go. His place was near ruint, the fences burnt, and the house would have been, but it was rock.... When the war was over, Massa come home and says, "You son of a gun, you's supposed to be free, but you ain't, 'cause I ain't gwine give you freedom." So I goes on working for him till I gits the chance to steal a hoss from him. The woman I wanted to marry, Govie, she 'cides to come to Texas with me. Me and Govie, we rides that hoss 'most a hundred miles, then we turned him a-loose and give him a scare back to his house, and come on foot the rest the way to Texas.

All we had to eat was what we could beg, and sometimes we went three days without a bite.... When we gits to Texas, we gits married [and] I settled on some land… There was some wild cattle and hogs, and that's the way we got our start, caught some of them and tamed them.

…I made bows and arrows to kill wild game with, and we never went to a store for nothing. We made our clothes out of animal skins.

Source: Toby Jones' description of freedom. Found in *Lay My Burden Down: A Folk History of Slavery*, Botkin, ed. Chicago: University of Chicago Press, 1945.

Summary:

After the war, I went on working for my master because he wouldn't let me go. After four years, I stole a horse. The woman I wanted to marry, Govie, went with me. We rode for a hundred miles, then sent the horse home. We walked the rest of the way to Texas.

In Texas we lived on the land. We tamed wild cattle and hogs. I made bows and arrows to kill wild game, and we never went to a store. We made our clothes from animal skins.

Vocabulary:

'ford = afford
gits = get
gwine = going

Afterword:
Some Ideas Change—
and Some Ideas Stay the Same

by Pat Perrin

In Europe, slavery was gradually replaced by other kinds of labor. Slavery, itself, had disappeared in England by the 1300s. However, under the feudal system, most workers were only slightly better off than slaves. These changes didn't reflect much difference in thinking.

Most Greeks, Romans, and Christians before the 16th century were able to defend slavery and feudal systems to their own satisfaction. But by the 18th century, European thinkers were turning to science and reasoning for answers.

In the period called the Enlightenment, writers defined new rights to freedom, happiness, and to the expression of ideas. They called for equality and justice for all. And that kind of thinking made it hard to claim that some people should be free and others should not. More and more, slavery began to seem both unnatural and immoral.

In the first half of the 1800s, the British ended slavery in their colonies—which put an end to it in many parts of the world. One country after another declared the slave trade illegal and also ended slavery in their own lands. For example, Chile freed its black slaves in 1823, Mexico abolished slavery in 1829, and Peru in 1854.

Obviously, Enlightenment thinking had a great effect on the American Declaration of Independence and the Constitution. But slavery was economically important to many of the states. It took a bitter war and a constitutional amendment to end it by 1865.

In a few countries, legal slavery continued into the 20th century. However, it probably exists nowhere legally now. Nevertheless, women and children are still bought and sold in some parts of the world. And some situations, such as the conditions of migrant workers, can be very much like slavery.

The ideas that made slavery possible—that some people are naturally superior, and that they're entitled to more rights than others—haven't completely disappeared. Those ideas shape some people's lives and produce various kinds of discrimination in our culture, even today.

Research Activities/Things to Do

- "Greatness does not come on flowery beds of ease to any people. We must fight to win the prize. No people to whom liberty is given, can hold it as firmly and wear it as grandly as those who wrench liberty from the iron hand of the tyrant. The hardships and dangers involved in the struggle give strength and toughness to the character, and enable it to stand firm in storm as well as in sunshine." (Frederick Douglass, *Life and Times of Frederick Douglass*) Explain why you agree or disagree with this statement by Frederick Douglass.

- Slaves who became sick with contagious diseases on the Middle Passage were thrown overboard, so that the crew or other slaves would not be infected. The slave traders were trying to protect their "assets." Each slave who died during the Middle Passage was a financial loss for the traders. Write an essay or a poem that describes how the traders valued money more than human life. Let the reader know what you think of that.

- Today, many African-Americans try to trace their ancestors' roots in Africa. What research methods would be most helpful in trying to find out more about people who were brought to this country as slaves, rather than coming here on their own?

Sample Written Document

Dayton, Ohio, August 7,1865

To My Old Master, Colonel P. H. Anderson
Big Spring, Tennessee

Sir: I got your letter and was glad to find you had not forgotten Jourdon, and that you wanted me to come back and live with you again, promising to do better for me than anybody else can. I have often felt uneasy about you.... Although you shot at me twice before I left you, I did not want to hear of your being hurt, and am glad you are still living....

I want to know particularly what the good chance is you propose to give me. I am doing tolerably well here; I get $25 a month, with victuals and clothing; have a comfortable home for Mandy (the folks here call her Mrs. Anderson), and the children. Milly, Jane and Grundy go to school and are learning well; the teacher says Grundy has a head for a preacher. They go to Sunday-School, and Mandy and me attend church regularly. We are kindly treated; sometimes we overhear others saying, "Them colored people were slaves" down in Tennessee. The children feel hurt when they hear such remarks, but I tell them it was no disgrace in Tennessee to belong to Col. Anderson. Many darkies would have been proud, as I used to was, to call you master. Now, if you will write and say what wages you will give me, I will be better able to decide whether it would be to my advantage to move back again.

As to my freedom, which you say I can have, there is nothing to be gained on that score, as I got my free-papers in 1864 from the Provost-Marshall-General of the Department at Nashville. Mandy says she would be afraid to go back without some proof that you are sincerely disposed to treat us justly and kindly—and we have concluded to test your sincerity by asking you to send us our wages for the time we served you. This will make us forget and forgive old scores, and rely on your justice and friendship in the future. I served you faithfully for thirty-two years and Mandy twenty years. At $25 a month for me, and $2 a week for Mandy, our earnings would amount to $11,680. Add to this the interest for the time our wages has been kept back and deduct what you paid for our clothing and three doctor's visits to me, and pulling a tooth for Mandy, and the balance will show what we are in justice entitled to.... If you fail to pay us for faithful labors in the past we can have little faith in your promises in the future. We trust the good Maker has opened your eyes to the wrongs which you and your fathers have done to me and my fathers, in making us toil for you for generations without recompense. Here I draw my wages every Saturday night, but in Tennessee there was never any pay day for the negroes any more than for the horses and cows. Surely there will be a day of reckoning for those who defraud the laborer of his hire.

In answering this letter please state if there would be any safety for my Milly and Jane, who are now grown up and both good-looking girls.... I would rather stay here and starve and die if it comes to that than have my girls brought to shame by the violence and wickedness of their young masters. You will also please state if there has been any schools opened for the colored children in your neighborhood, the great desire of my life now is to give my children an education, and have them form virtuous habits....

From your old servant, Jourdon Anderson

Written Document Worksheet

Based on Worksheet from *Teaching with Documents*,
National Archives and Records Administration

1. **Type of document:**

   ❏ Newspaper   ❏ Diary   ❏ Advertisement

   ❏ Letter   ❏ Patent   ❏ Telegram

   ❏ Deed   ❏ Ship Manifest   ❏ Census Report

   ❏ Press Release   ❏ Journal   ❏ Memo

   ❏ Congressional Record   ❏ Report   ❏ Other_____

   ❏ Transcript from Oral History

2. **Unique Characteristics of the Document:**

   ❏ Interesting Stationery   ❏ "RECEIVED" Stamp

   ❏ Unusual Fold Marks   ❏ "TOP SECRET" Stamp

   ❏ Handwritten   ❏ "CLASSIFIED" Stamp

   ❏ Written Notations   ❏ "Copy"

   ❏ Typed   ❏ Official

   ❏ Other Stamp_____

3. **Date(s) of Document:**   ❏ No Date

4. **Author of Document:**   **Position:**

5. **For what audience was the document written?**

6. **Key Information** *(In your opinion, what are the 3 most important points of the document?)*

   a.

   b.

   c.

7. **Why do you think the document was written?**

8. **Choose a quote from the document that helped you to know why it was written:**

- The Nat Turner revolt in 1831 crystallized white southern fears about larger slave rebellions, and touched upon the most sensitive feelings of white racism in the South. How does the poet explain the strains and pressures the Nat Turner revolt placed upon plantation life?

Source: *American Imprints.* Copyright, Ken Siegelman, Modern Images Poet Committee, Brooklyn, NY, 1994.

NAT TURNER
by Ken Siegelman

Its name came to mind
In worried looks
Passed in silence
Between the overseer in the fields
And the gentleman
In the Big House —
Slowly they began
To count the knives
After every meal;
numbering sickles, scythes
And hatchets
In the tool sheds,
Before the twilight
Cast the Southern landscape
In the uncertainty of betrayal...
They took to questioning
Slaves they never took much notice of,
With the feigned gentility
Of smiling concern —
Waiting for the signs
Of a swallowed lie
From young girls
Who seemed to take too long
In making up the rooms,
And field hands
Who took ill
On the same day
Without warning.

- The Dred Scott Case (1857) was a setback for the abolition of slavery. Dred Scott, a slave, was taken by his master into the free states of Illinois, Wisconsin, and Minnesota. For four years, Scott stayed out of Missouri, the slave state he had lived in with his previous owner. He believed that he should be considered a free man because he had established himself as a free person on "free soil." The lower courts ruled against Scott. The case then went to the Supreme Court of the United States, which also ruled unfavorably. All but two of the justices agreed that "Dred Scott could not bring suit in federal court because he was a Negro, not just a slave. No Negro, whether slave or free, could ever be considered a citizen of the United States within the meaning of the Constitution." Opponents to the decision were outraged. Find out what you can about the case and about the speakers announced on the poster below.

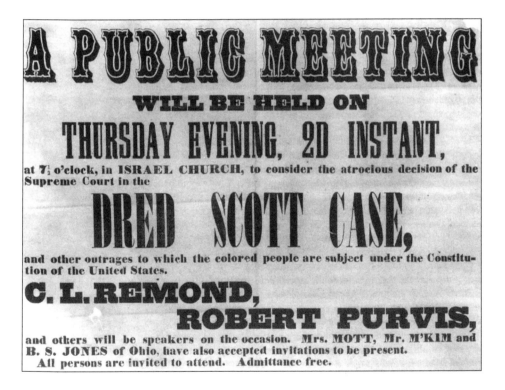

- William Lloyd Garrison was one of the most vocal whites in the abolition movement. In his newspaper, *The Liberator*, he demanded unconditional and immediate emancipation of all slaves. He worked toward that end from 1830 until the ratification of the Thirteenth Amendment in 1865. How did Garrison use the Declaration of Independence to further his cause?

Suggested Further Reading

Companion Literature Compiled by Ellin Rossberg

The books listed below are suggested readings in American literature, which tie in with the *Researching American History Series.*

Colonial Triangular Trade

The Captive, Joyce Hanson - M
Middle Passage, Charles Johnson - HS
The Slave Dancer, Paula Fox - M
Jump Ship to Freedom, James Lincoln Collier and Christopher Collier - M
Classic Slave Narratives, Henry Louis Gates, Jr., editor - HS (nonfiction)
Slave Ship (original title: *The Long Black Schooner*), Emma Gelders Sterne - M
Confessions of Nat Turner, William Styron - M
Nightjohn, Gary Paulsen - M (reading level)/HS (subject matter)
Middle Passage: White Ships, Black Cargo, Tom Feelings - HS (graphic narrative)
Colonial Triangular Trade: An Economy Based on Human Misery, Phyllis Raybin
  Emert - M/HS (nonfiction)

Reconstruction

Amos Fortune: Free Man, Elizabeth Yates - EL/M
Shades of Gray, Carolyn Reeder - M
Out from This Place, Joyce Hanson - M (sequel to Which Way Freedom)
The Autobiography of Miss Jane Pittman, Ernest J. Gaines - HS
Souls of Black Folk, W.E.B. DuBois - HS (nonfiction)
Gone with the Wind, Margaret Mitchell - HS
Reconstruction: Binding the Wounds, Cheryl Edwards - nonfiction - M/HS

The Underground Railroad

Which Way Freedom, Joyce Hanson - M
Underground Man, Milton Meltzer - M
Long Journey Home, Julius Lester - M
Harriet Tubman: Conductor on the Underground Railroad, Ann Petry - EL/M
Brady, Jean Fritz -EL/M
Nightjohn, Gary Paulsen - M
Freedom Crossing, Margaret Goff Clark - M
A Girl Called Boy, Belinda Humerce - M
Jayhawker, Patricia Beatty - EL/M
School for Pompey Walker, Michael Walker - EL/M
Classic Slave Narratives, Henry Louis Gates, Jr., ed. - HS (nonfiction)
The Underground Railroad: Life on the Road to Freedom, Pat Perrin - M/HS
  (nonfiction)

For information on these and other titles from Discovery Enterprises, Ltd., call or write to: Discovery Enterprises, Ltd., 31 Laurelwood Drive, Carlisle, MA 01741 Phone: 978-287-5401 Fax: 978-287-5402